HOW DID THIS HAPPEN TO ME?

HOW DID THIS HAPPEN TO ME?

GR8 RELATIONSHIPS

EQUIP PRESS

Colorado Springs

HOW DID THIS HAPPEN TO ME?

Published by Equip Press, Colorado Springs, CO

First Edition: 2022
How Did This Happen To Me? / GR8 Relationships
Paperback ISBN: 978-1-958585-11-5
eBook ISBN:978-1-958585-14-6

EQUIP PRESS

Colorado Springs

CONTENTS

Hermann and Louie's Story   **9**

  Hermann   9

  Louie   18

Who is to Blame?   **25**

  What is The Problem?   25

  What is The Solution?   25

  The Flashing ME   26

    Are you Acting Like a Baby?   27

    A Better Question   29

  Will You Be Served by Others or Serve Others?   31

  Love Versus Selfishness   32

What Breaks Down?   **37**

  Feelings   37

    Feelings Can Create Problems   40

    Feelings and Behavior   42

  Freedom   44

    Freedom Defined   46

    Irresponsible Freedom   48

  Forgiveness   50

    Guilt is the Problem   52

  Confession   57

What is the Best ME?   **61**

  Feelings   62

    Act the Way You Want to Feel   63

    Help Attitudes Change   66

    Thinking/Feeling Principle   67

  Freedom   72

    Freedom – Great for Relationships   73

    Responsible Freedom   73

    Freedom Is Divine   74

Forgiveness 79
   Forgiveness Pleases God 79
   Forgiveness Imitates God 79
   Forgiveness Escapes Serious Consequences 80
   Your Choice 80
Forgiveness Process 82
   Step One: Stop the Bleeding – Face Your Humanity 84
   Step Two: Clean the Wound – Overlook Revenge 85
   Step Three: Apply Antibiotic – Renew Your Mind 86
   Step Four: Cover the Wound – Give it Up,
     Grasp it No More 88
   Step Five: Change the Dressing Regularly –
     Apply Your Decision 91
   Step Six: Look for Signs of Infection –
     Validate and Verify Your Decision 92
   Step Seven: Enjoy Healing – and Freedom 94
Confession Process 97
   Step One: Choose Humility 97
   Step Two: Own Your Guilt. Do Not Excuse It. 98
   Step Three: Name the Real Offense 99
   Step Four: Feel the Offense as they Felt It 100
   Step Five: Earnestly Repent of your Sin 100
   Step Six: Soberly Confess your Sin 101
   Step Seven: Sincerely Thank God for the Conflict 101

Epilogue **105**

Study Guide **107**
Scripture Meditation 107
Who's to Blame? 108
What Breaks Down? 110
What is the Best ME? 112
Forgiveness Exercise 114

Tools **115**

Endnotes **123**

HOW DID THIS HAPPEN TO ME?!

Has your world been rocked by an event you didn't expect? Are you reeling from a hurt relationship or someone walking out on you? Sometimes traumatic events shock you into action in order to move you toward a corrected or more excellent path in life.

This book and these sessions are designed to:

- Help you discover why your life surprised you. What is it that you missed that allowed the destruction in an important relationship?
- Inform you of the damage caused by misguidance and misunderstanding regarding Feelings, Freedom, Forgiveness and Confession.
- Show you how to use Feelings, Freedom, Forgiveness and Confession in ways that are constructive and life-giving.

Why was the GR8 Relationships Training Born?

The GR8 Relationships ministry started with a painful and poignant tipping point in founder Hermann Eben's life. Hermann confesses, "It honestly took me by surprise. I was not a victim in the scenario, but it was a slap in the face that woke me up to so much about me, my wife, and our relationship. It caused me to look at my relationship with God more closely, too."

HERMANN AND LOUIE'S STORY[1]

Every relationship has two perspectives on the story, since at least two people are involved, and they view situations differently, from their own lens. As you observe the perspectives of this opening story, reflect on how you relate to it. What do you identify with and what makes you shudder at the memory of something in your own life that knocked you off your feet?

Hermann

You can categorize moments in your life by looking for times of happiness, sorrow, anger, discouragement, or even peace. Generally, the moments that are the most vivid create the greatest chance for change and learning.

For me, three vivid times where I cried because of a major epiphany marked specific learning events in my life in 1981, 1991, and 1999. Each one of the events are still vivid in my memory.

1981

The event in 1981 is relatively short, and when I meditate on it I can still see and feel the way it happened. I was on a long flight coming back home and was preparing to teach that coming Sunday. For some reason, the Lord brought Psalm 42:1 to my mind. It was not related to the passage I was teaching, but it was a verse that I had memorized earlier in my life.

> *As the deer pants for the water brooks, So pants my soul for You, O God.*

Psalm 42:1, NKJV

At that point in time, I realized that I did not pant after God. Instead, I made life all about me. It became so clear to me that I started crying. It was so clear to me that I was studying and teaching God's word for my own benefit, to look good to others, to be knowledgeable about His word more than experience the amazing relationship we can have with the Lord.

As I have reflected on that time, clearly, God was getting my attention to prepare me for future events in my life. It was almost as if He were saying, "Knowing My Word is great for you, but you will need a strong relationship with Me for some future events that I have for you."

So that time of crying was more about the Lord showing and preparing me for 1991 and 1999. While I did not know it then, He was telling me to pay attention to Him, learn about Him in a fuller and deeper way rather than just having knowledge about Him.

1991

The second time I cried was in 1991. Louie and I refer to this as the *blow up* because things really exploded in our marriage. I have specific, clear memories of what happened in late September, 1991. Amazingly, I cannot remember the exact day, but I think it was a Wednesday. I was in my office, the phone rang, and I answered it. The person on the other end clearly said, "Your wife is having an affair. Do you want evidence of that?"

My angry response was, "You've got to be kidding me! Who is this? Who is joking with me? Who's telling me this?" There was a pause and I said, "You really want me to believe this?"

"Yes, I'm telling you the truth."

"Well, I don't believe you!" and I hung up.

They called back and said, "Do you want evidence of this?"

Annoyed, I replied, "Whatever you want to do, do it, but do not call back."

As I reflected on the call, I realized what the caller said could be true based on where our relationship was.

Primarily, it could be true based on the way that I had been treating Louie. It definitely could be true based on how often her behavior and actions annoyed me. But obviously I did not want it to be true. The pain of just hearing those words was real, despite my anger at the caller for saying them. I did not want it to be true, but reality was against me.

Reality paid me a visit about three days later. My assistant brought me the mail and placed it in my inbox. One item, a small package, stood out. I noticed scrawled writing on it that said, "Personal for Hermann Eben." As I looked at the package, I felt nervous and even fearful. Was this the evidence from that phone call?

But I did not open the package, because that is not the "Hermann Eben" way. I was not going to let that package interfere with everything I needed to do and there was a lot of work that day. That is my typical method of operating: persevere with what needs to be done and eliminate distractions. Of course, in this instance it was easier for me to ignore the package in hope that it was not what I feared.

So, the package just sat there. I looked at it occasionally, but I did not even want to touch it because I knew I had to do other things. Finally, at the end of the day, I stopped and looked at the package.

I opened it and pulled out a cassette tape. Since I did not have a tape player in my office, I started looking for one. The company spanned eight floors and since it was late at night, and everyone was gone, I searched until I found a tape player on the third floor. I unplugged it, took it to my office, shut the door, plugged it in, and started listening.

What I heard is painful to repeat even now, years later. I heard a conversation between my dear wife and another man about how she loved him, not me. Obviously, I was emotional and upset. I sat and thought and finally decided to call my pastor, Fred Lybrand. I was an elder at the church, so we had a particularly good relationship.

When I got him on the phone I said, "I've got some really bad news. I need your help."

Just asking for help was vastly different and not easy for me because Hermann Eben always did things on his own. Normally, I did not think I needed help. As evidence, my treatment of Louie was likely part of that type of thinking.

He immediately came down to my office. We talked and decided to call Dr. Marlin Howe. He was probably the best alternative for us, since we knew how he thought about marriage and relationships. The church had been using his *Hope for Relationships* video series for about five years and each of the elders led the weekend workshops.

We called him, and he agreed to work with us all weekend starting Friday morning.

Everything was a blur between Wednesday night and Friday morning. One thing that was easy to remember is my anger toward Louie. That Wednesday was one of the few times that I remember literally yelling at her after confronting her with the evidence.

When Friday came, it was tough on both Louie and me. Interestingly, Dr. Howe saw both of us as the problem, not just Louie. He was tough on me and tough on Louie. The only details of the conversation that weekend that come to mind happened on Friday afternoon. It is one of the most memorable parts of the weekend for me, and it was another point of crying. (The event is so important because in the GR8 Relationships, it is what we now view as the first step in forgiveness.)

When Dr. Howe talked to each of us, it was mostly with both of us present so we could hear firsthand what was said. When he was talking to Louie, she admitted what she had done, which stirred my anger even more.

As he continued to question her I thought, "There's more to this story that you aren't telling. Why don't you just tell the whole truth about your life!"

Obviously, I had a bad attitude toward her. But the most memorable and impactful part of the weekend for me was about to happen. As Dr. Howe continued to question her, I realized how judgmental I was toward her and how much that was true of other relationships in my life.

As I began to realize these things about myself, Dr. Howe started questioning Louie more intensely about what other things she needed to confess. Then she started crying, and she does not tend to cry often. She seemed like she was at her wit's end.

As she was crying, she looked at Dr. Howe, raised her hands palms up like she was showing God her hands and said, "Lord, you know that I am clean. I don't have anything else to confess."

At that point I saw her humanity again. I was not looking at her through the eyes of what she had done to me. I saw the face of her humanity. I saw her as broken human being like I am. She was a person to me again.

When she raised her arms and her hands to the Lord, it was like the Lord speaking to me, "Hermann, stop being so judgmental. You are broken, too."

Forgiveness came into our lives in a real (and different) way. From that weekend wonderful healing was almost immediate. There were also some exceedingly difficult times, like when both of us publicly resigned our positions at the church. I was asked to stand in front of the church and resign as an elder, and Louie was by my side. Louie was required to publicly resign as the teaching director of Community Bible Study, in front of about 300 ladies she had been teaching weekly.

Trying to understand how forgiveness works took me a lot of time and thought. For sure, it was not an overnight miracle where happily-ever-after started. For example, I remember a time six months later, when I went to the grocery store and Louie stayed home. One of the things Dr. Howe asked us to do was invite the other person to go when we were going to the store or running an errand. But this was one time that Louie was not with me.

This did not become a crying situation, but it created real panic in me. It is also a great example of how your feelings are untrustworthy, and how you can let them become a real problem due to your bad thinking. There, at the store it seemed like it came out of nowhere; it could have been Satan putting thoughts in my head, but I became convinced that Louie had left me. I just knew it. (And remember, this is six months later.) Something in my mind, probably Satan, was telling me that when I got back home, she was not going to be there.

You can imagine the panic that ran through me. I do not remember whether I checked out or I just left my items at the store. I do know that I went home immediately, drove into the garage, and her car was there. Then I ran into the house and called for her, and thankfully, she was still there. She was not gone like I was thinking.

At that point there was some crying, hugging her, and saying, "You are here! I just had a panic attack thinking you were gone."

So, 1981 was a time that the Lord said "you have made life about yourself, not about Me." Then in 1991 the Lord showed me that I had made life about me not about Louie and the family.

1999

Finally, 1999 was the time I cried because I finally realized how controlling and judgmental I am or, hopefully, was. This event gave me more clarity on how much I had been driving Louie, the kids, and others away from me because of my controlling nature. Without getting into the details, I cried because I realized how much I continued to control and judge others. That is just another form making life about me.

It is like saying, "You don't understand how things work like I do. You are doing it wrong unless you are doing it my way."

Being so controlling and judgmental ignores the power of freedom for me and for others. This is a big truth that is part of the GR8 Relationships message.

So, crying has been a mechanism for learning in my life. That probably is not what you would expect me to say, but each situation has been an incredibly good experience to encourage humility, of which I need more. As you can see in those three situations, this principle is demonstrated: first humiliation, then humility.

Louie

As you can see from our story, for all intents and purposes (and especially by worldly standards) our marriage would be over had we not begun to practice the principles in God's Word that are outlined in GR8 Relationships. We would either be divorced—well, maybe not divorced since that was not an option for us—we might have killed each other (murder, yes, but not divorce!).

I supposed at best we would be two miserable creatures living under one roof. But it is God's grace that enlightened me with the idea that relationships are how we work out our salvation. When you stop to think about it, if we were just living by ourselves on a deserted island, yes, we could have a relationship with the Lord, but there are so many biblical principles that we learn, and they all have to do with relationships with each other. Relationships are how we practice these biblical principles.

The marital relationship is the most important because it displays the full image of God, but all our other relationships are very key and valuable to our lives. One of the verses that Dr. Howe uses in his video series set my life in a different direction. I am sure I had heard it before, but it didn't really impact me. He uses this scripture from Philippians.

> *Let each of you look out not only for his own interests, but also for the interests of others.*

Philippians 2:4, NKJV

This requires considering our relationships with others. How can I honestly and truly serve Christ with a good spirit, right motivation, and a right heart unless I am doing that in my relationships? The way we live in relationships is an indication of how we relate to God.

These principles Hermann and I try to practice have been invaluable to our relationship, and our relationship today is absolutely incredible. So much so that sometimes I feel guilty for being content.

And I will have to say, too, what a privilege and honor to continue the work that Marlin and Patty Howe started. And even though it is not always comfortable to share our junk, I know that is where God has placed us and what He wants us to do because it has helped and ministered to so many people. With that said, let me add some elements of my story.

I put my trust in Christ at an early age, but really did not put what I knew into practice until my adult life. Some of you can relate to the fact that it seems like we grow the most during the times that are the hardest, because we begin to get a sense of really how helpless we are during those times. So, we depend on God the most during those times.

We have had struggles in our life, but as usual, a few things have just been huge. One of those is the loss of our firstborn. I understand that God allows those things to happen, and yet it was really hard for me to deal with that pain

The other thing that happened was after Hermann and I had been married for 20 years I realized that our relationship just really stunk. I became very rebellious because Herman was not meeting my expectations. Of course, it did not occur to me that maybe I needed to change, not Hermann.

Another big issue that added to the problem was my addiction to alcohol. I did not realize it was an addiction at the time, but I have really struggled with alcohol.

As I looked back over those times such as the loss of our child, I would drink to cover up my emotions, those things I did not want to feel. Of course, those emotions did not leave. Drinking did not help except maybe temporarily. But it did not make the pain go away.

Of course, the same was true of our marriage and my unfaithfulness to Hermann. Over the years, I knew God had forgiven me, and I knew that Hermann had forgiven me but there was still a feeling of guilt and shame that was hard to move past.

Over time it became really evident that I depended on alcohol to mask my emotions rather than depending on Christ to remove them. I did not see life for what it is and believe that Christ had forgiven me. So, once again, I turned to alcohol to mask those feelings rather than turning to the Lord.

The every-once-in-a-while drinking turned into full-blown addiction, and it was not working for me anymore. It did not take away the feelings that I had. The bad emotions did not leave. And praise the Lord, through other circumstances, He clearly showed me that I had a problem.

Through God's grace and Hermann's patience I began to get help with my addiction. Hermann was not very patient about it at first, but later, because of his understanding of freedom, he left me to my own devices. That left me with nobody to blame but myself. Then, I recognized I was responsible for my actions. I could not blame Hermann's mistreatment of me because he was nothing but kind and loving. I had to face the music, as they say.

Over the years God continues to heal me. Working through biblical principles, understanding God's forgiveness, the freedom that He has given me in my life, and seeing Hermann for who he is and the man that God has made him to be, have all been part of that healing. I believe that Hermann loves me today. God continues to bless us as we confess and forgive.

God has blessed us with three beautiful grown children and seven grandchildren. And God also continues to give me daily reprieve of my alcohol addiction. Our marriage is just the best!

REFLECTIVE QUESTIONS

1. What resonated with you about Hermann and
    Louie's story?

    _____

    _____

    _____

    _____

    _____

2. What did you identify with?

    _____

    _____

    _____

    _____

    _____

    _____

3. How do you feel this scripture applies to life right
    now? What keeps you from panting after God?

    *As the deer pants for the water brooks, So pants
    my soul for You, O God.*

    Psalm 42:1, NKJV

_____

_____

_____

_____

_____

_____

WHO IS
TO BLAME?

If there is someone to blame in a relationship, does that mean there is a problem? The answer is probably yes. Let's take a look at the problem, and if there is a solution.

What is The Problem?

Isn't it obvious that the problem is them? No!

The problem in relationships occurs when you make everything about yourself. Have you ever heard yourself say, imply, or think any of the following?

"You need to do it my way."

"You need to make me happy."

"You need to change." (I am okay, you aren't!)

What is The Solution?

The solution is simple: Turn your focus away from yourself and pursue the best for others. Do this patiently, kindly, sacrificially, and unconditionally.

This sounds simple enough, so why is it so difficult to turn and embrace pursuing their best? At GR8 Relationships, we call the problem *The Flashing ME*.

The Flashing ME

The *Flashing ME* can be, and probably is, your biggest problem. The meaning is what it sounds like. Your *Me* is your focus. It demands that you serve yourself, demand your way and focus on yourself more than focusing on or serving others.

The fact that you may not see how often you focus on yourself (that is, on *ME*) is a sad thought. You notice when other people are selfish and self-absorbed, but not when you do it. Is that true for you? It is for me.

When others are selfish it is like they have the word *ME* flashing on their forehead. But when you do it, you cannot see it because it is on your forehead above your eyes. You can be totally selfish, not interested in serving others, which means your *ME* is flashing bright enough to light a house, but you do not see it. You can look at this another way and ask yourself if you are acting like a baby.

Are you Acting Like a Baby?

A baby is a good picture of how the problem works. Not the picture of a baby cuddly and innocent, but an out-of-control, screaming infant who wants something, just because they do. That's another good name for the problem: The Baby.

Simply put, the Baby plugs into the sin nature, which is plugged into the world, which is ruled by Satan himself. As the Baby, you take everything personally, which makes your *ME* flash.

Defensiveness is the primary reaction of The Baby, especially when you are criticized. You live primarily by appetites, impulses, and pleasures. You focus on selfishness, self-absorption, and self-sufficiency; "it's all about *ME*."

This problem is built-in and is part of everyone. Those without the life of Christ and the Spirit of God in them are slaves to that *ME* behavior.

Those of us who have trusted Jesus's death, burial, and resurrection as the answer for our sin have a fundamental choice: trust God or trust something or someone other than God. Present yourself to righteousness or unrighteousness, as it says in Romans.

> *And do not present your members as instruments of unrighteousness to sin but present yourselves to God as being alive from the dead, and your members as instruments of righteousness to God.*

Romans 6:13, NKJV

Most people act like The Baby.

You have built-in desires including being accepted, feeling included, significant, valuable, close, secure, safe, cared for, and satisfied. When you fear you will not get those, and others like them, your *ME* starts flashing. But admitting your tendency to be self-absorbed is not easy. You will excuse your behavior with statements like "If I don't look out for myself, who will?"

Self-absorption does not need to be chosen. That mindset or behavior is the default of our sin nature, or a life that trusts something other than God. The chart below shows the human nature tendency to certain actions and mindsets based on our sin nature, which is self-focused rather than other-focused. The right side of the chart gives some solutions to deal with our natural tendencies.

Make everything about me	
THINKING ACTION	SOLUTION
Be defensive	Be teachable
Be self-absorbed	Be considerate
Be self-indulgent	Be self-controlled
Work on your self-esteem	Accept who you are
Be a victim	Make choices
Always be right	Seek truth
Seek revenge	Forgive
Be manipulative	Tell the truth
React and respond	Choose and create
Be unilateral, self-serving	Pursue others' best

A Better Question

Since flashing your ME comes from your sin nature you must choose to act differently. That will only happen with the energy of the Holy Spirit. It is impossible for the sin nature to choose against itself.

Here is a way to see if you are flashing your *ME*: any time you are irritable, discontent, discouraged, depressed, or angry, you can ask yourself this simple question, "Am I making this about me right now?"

That is no longer an experiment for me. I know how self-absorbed I am. In fact, for about eight years (starting in 2001) I did exactly what I just asked you to do. After asking that question for all those years, I stopped one day and tried to think of a time that I had honestly answered, "No, I am not making this about ME." I could not remember one time where I could honestly answer no. While I am probably more selfish than you, please try the exercise. More than likely, it will reveal results that surprise you.

Because of that personal research and the tendency to not be objective, here is a better question when you have those negative emotions, "How am I making this about ME right now?" That is a much better question because you most likely are making everything about ME, so just start looking for *how* you are doing it this time.

Realizing that I have negative emotions has been a reliable tool to alert me to my selfish behavior. Being a Baby is the problem for all relationships. Based on God's Word, it is a serious problem. Please memorize the following verses to remind yourself how damaging the problem is for you and others.

> *For where envy and self-seeking exist, confusion and every evil thing are there.*

James 3:16, NKJV

> *So they come to you as people do, they sit before you as My people, and they hear your words, but they do not do them; for with their mouth they show much love, but their hearts pursue their own gain.*

Ezekiel 33:31, NKJV

Will You Be Served by Others or Serve Others?

A basic question that will help you identify when your *ME* is flashing is to think about whether you expect others to serve your wants and needs, or you expect to serve others and tend to their needs. In a way this is at the heart love.

If we think about our savior Jesus, who put our needs before His own, the picture of true love emerges. Did he dread being dragged to Calvary to be crucified? The scripture says He even agonized whether His plight could be avoided.

> *He went a little farther and fell on His face, and prayed, saying, "O My Father, if it is possible, let this cup pass from Me; nevertheless, not as I will, but as You will."*

Matthew 26:39, NKJV

Jesus prayed this prayer three times. In spite of the pain He knew He would endure, He *chose* to die for others, for you and me, to replace us and our sin by dying on the cross. That is an ultimate example of love.

Love Versus Selfishness

Love and selfishness are opposites, and enemies, because they are representative of God and Satan. God is love and Satan is about pride, self-absorption, and flashing *ME*. Satan continually seeks his own way rather than depend on God. On the other hand, love never seeks to hurt or neglect others. It strives for others' welfare, satisfaction, and advantage. It pursues their highest good. And the outstanding benefit is satisfaction and fulfillment for the one who loves.

Consider this scenario. You are selfish and self-absorbed looking to be satisfied. You indulge in your appetites, impulses and pleasures and are satisfied. Since the fulfillment was based on something that was temporary by nature, it can only provide what its nature allows or is. Eating a piece of chocolate provides temporary fulfillment because it is temporary in its nature. Indulging in materialism, sex, drugs, alcohol can only provide temporary satisfaction due to their physical, temporal properties.

Worse yet, the dependence on the temporary item easily escalates, because you want the satisfaction again. But the object of the satisfaction is temporary by nature and invariably produces less rather than more satisfaction as you rely on it. You can continue to escalate the reliance on it or allow your appetites, impulses, and pleasures to drive you into something that promises more satisfaction. But the satisfaction is built on temporal, deceptive elements and it eventually collapses. You desire satisfaction but ultimately it is unrealized.

Satisfaction is dependent on the nature of the object trusted to provide satisfaction. If you are dependent on a person acknowledging how much you helped them, you are depending on a faulty source. If you trust in God's very nature, His perfection, and trustworthiness, you will be satisfied every time you do what He wants you to do. He is the living water, contrasted to the earthly water that satisfies for a while then satisfies less the more you drink. You always have to return because its ability to satisfy wears off.

When you learn to put all your emotions and pleasure in doing what God asks, you will experience true satisfaction. It is a satisfaction no longer dependent on life, circumstances, or people.

Are you like Jesus, serving others in spite of your personal suffering and pain? Or, are you like the world, focusing on you and your needs despite what others around you need?

<u>REFLECTIVE QUESTIONS</u>

1. Describe a time when you have noticed your
    Flashing ME.

    _____

    _____

    _____

    _____

    _____

2. In the situation you described above, how could
    you have focused on pursuing the best for others?

    _____

    _____

    _____

    _____

    _____

3. How do you see this scripture applying to
    relationships?

    *For where envy and self-seeking exist, confusion
    and every evil thing are there.*

    James 3:16, NKJV

_____

_____

_____

_____

_____

4. The next time you see your *Flashing ME*, what will
   you do differently?

_____

_____

_____

_____

_____

WHAT BREAKS DOWN?

Okay, I recognize that my *ME* is Flashing. Now what? My relationship still has hurts and problems. What am I supposed to do?

Forgiveness and confession are the two critical tools required for a great relationship.

Yet, in counseling sessions, often people say, "I just don't *feel* like confessing or forgiving."

"I didn't do anything wrong, so I am not confessing."

"I can't ever forgive him for what he did to me."

People have some misconceptions about relationships and life. In the GR8 Relationships, we talk about the *Three Fs and a C* – Feelings, Freedom, Forgiveness, and Confession. Let's explore each of these and how they truly work, then in a later section, we'll explore how to use them as tools in relationships.

Feelings

The first F represents Feelings. Feelings are too often the standard used by people to determine whether they or others are doing okay. As you will see, that creates problems. In fact, too much of the time, people's feelings are using them rather than the person using their feelings in a constructive way. Let's look at how feelings work.

Do you have a favorite scary movie? Maybe the classic *Psycho*? Or possibly a more modern one like the *Scream* series? Mine is the original *Alien*. Even though it is my favorite, I don't like to watch it because it does such a good job of scaring me with the special effects and creatures.

Why are you afraid when you watch a scary movie? When something scary happens on the screen, why do you jump? Is it because you are in danger? Or course not. It is just a movie.

Suppose you are watching a scary movie, but you tell yourself, "I'm watching a story filmed for entertainment, especially to create fear and excitement. Scenes in the movie are designed to scare me, but I know that it is not really happening to me."

Wouldn't that take all the fun out of the movie?

The film is structured to draw you into the story, to appeal to your emotions making you see yourself as one of the characters in the movie. When you remind yourself of reality, the fear is reduced, or removed. Your emotions are primarily responding to your thinking, therefore reducing the film's efforts to engage your fear. We can conclude two key factors from this.

First, feelings and emotions are primarily *responders*. When you watch a movie and you feel scared, sad or happy, or actually cry, your emotions are responding to the movie. Feelings need something to respond to.

Second, and most important, feelings are often *untrustworthy*. If you can feel scared even though you are not in danger, like you might feel watching a scary movie, then your emotions are not trustworthy. Your emotions are real, but they are responding to something that is not real.

That is why when you tell yourself, "It's just a movie," your emotions are reduced or removed; they are responding to your thinking.

With that in mind, consider these three words: Think, Feel and Act. Which sequence do you suppose most people use? How about you?

Like it or not, people typically react and respond like an amoeba, a single cell organism that has little or no ability to think. Poke it, and it will move away. Offer sugar, and it will come to you.

Before going any further, I need to state that I believe emotions and feelings are great! The proper use of emotion allows us to enjoy the highs and lows of life. The danger occurs when you trust your emotions to initiate actions but do not look for what your emotions were responding to.

Feelings Can Create Problems

Trusting your feelings is not a great strategy. Again, it is not that feelings are bad, they are just indicators. They respond to the stimuli they receive and are, therefore, untrustworthy, and fickle. You can validate that your feelings are primarily responders and often untrustworthy by considering two simple statements:

- Bad can feel good
- Good can feel bad

Bad can feel good is easy to prove. You have no doubt experienced feeling good, even excited, as you encounter temptation and sin. But it is followed by an inner conviction that you have done something wrong. That good feeling about doing something bad will always be temporary, unless your heart is hardened.

Vengeance is one *bad* that may feel good longer than other sins, because your mind is focused on justice and getting even. Most other sins register quickly with regret or guilt replacing whatever positive emotion was there. The story of any sin fits the "bad can feel good" statement and is clearly illustrated in the original sin in the Garden of Eden.

> *So when the woman saw that the tree was good*
> *for food, that it was pleasant to the eyes, and*
> *a tree desirable to make one wise, she took of*
> *its fruit and ate. She also gave to her husband*

with her, and he ate. Then the eyes of both of them were opened, and they knew that they were naked; and they sewed fig leaves together and made themselves coverings.

And they heard the sound of the LORD God walking in the garden in the cool of the day, and Adam and his wife hid themselves from the presence of the LORD God among the trees of the garden.

Genesis 3:6–8, NKJV

Put yourself in Eve's place and let your emotions follow the story. Eve was swept away by the appeal of the fruit: good for food, pleasant to the eyes, could make her wise – so she ate. It sounds very much like she felt good about eating the fruit, but it was bad. And to prove it was bad, notice where Adam and Eve's feelings go next. "Their eyes were opened . . . knew they were naked . . . hid themselves…" Feelings were responding to the reality of what God said would happen.

Most often, the good feelings happen prior to and during the sin, because you do not listen to the conviction of our conscience or the Holy Spirit saying, "Think about this! Don't do it!"

Good can feel bad is also real. Consider the emotional conflict you experience when you know a close friend or relative is sinning. You are clear that it is time to speak with them, so you gather your courage to do it, but your emotions work against you. And, in those cases where the conversation goes poorly, you may experience feelings of regret instead of peace or joy for doing what was right.

A good parent disciplining their child understands *good can feel bad.* Similarly, when a good leader shares the truth with a person because they are not doing a good job, it often does not feel good.

Consider the following:

Just because I do right does not mean I will feel right at that time. The corollary: just because I feel right does not mean I am doing right.

Finally, God's Word says it best.

> *There is a way that seems right to a man,*
> *but in the end it leads to death.*

Proverbs 16:25, NKJV

Feelings and Behavior

Since your feelings are only indicators or responders, then either acting or thinking should come first. You would think that choice is easy, right? But many people choose: Ready – Fire – Aim. If you are shooting a gun at a target, that is not a good option. You are acting before you think, which is seldom a good option. In fact, I speculate that no one does that, just like no one actually follows their heart or follows their emotions. I realize that statement needs more explanation, but just hold the tension for now.

No doubt, thinking belongs at the beginning, so should acting come second or third?

What is the connection between feelings and behavior? Do your feelings impact your behavior? Does your behavior impact your feelings?

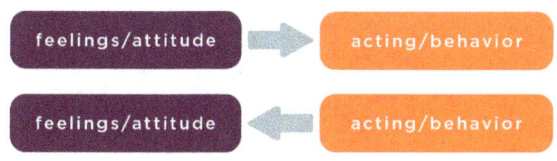

The answer is yes, both happen. It is easy to see that feelings drive behaviors, but the opposite is true also. For example, researchers have consistently found that people who are behaving in ways that conflict with their feelings or attitude will change their feelings to be more consistent with their behavior. That is why people who have gone through the trauma of having an arm or leg amputated are often asked to go help others in the hospital as soon as they can do so.

It is easy to have misconceptions about feelings and how they work because that is what the world and

Satan want you to believe. But that is not what the Bible teaches you. Later in the book we'll explore how to use feelings in a positive and constructive way.

Freedom

The second F is Freedom. Freedom can be both responsible and irresponsible. Understanding the difference is crucial in developing great relationships. The way you view and employ freedom impacts your use of the other F's and the C: feelings, forgiveness, and confession. Freedom is often difficult to understand. Misunderstanding regarding what true freedom means can cripple relationships and seldom helps them.

Consider this scenario. A husband and father of four plays golf every Saturday morning with his buddies. He feels he deserves it because he is a traveling executive, always under pressure to provide for his wife and children and he needs time to relax, to not think about all his responsibilities. His wife is tired at the end of the week after tending to their home, yard, and the kids and all their activities. She has shared with him on more than one occasion that she needs a break, too, and would like to take a Saturday off occasionally to relax and do something fun with him. He doesn't ever do anything to change his pattern. When she brings it up, he is all too quick to remind her that she does not have to work, and she should appreciate the privileged life she has. He then will promise a romantic vacation to Hawaii without the kids, but he never seems to be able to get away from work long enough to do that.

She avoids the subject because of the lecture about how *easy* she has it. It just isn't worth it. She always walks away from the conversation feeling unvalued. Months grow into years and, trying to be the good wife and avoiding the uncomfortable conversation, she says nothing, but deep inside she feels abandoned, like he is not recognizing what she contributes to the family. Eventually she finds herself angry and resentful of his weekly golf outings. Finally, she gives him an ultimatum, that she will not cook for him on the weekends that he is playing golf. She takes the kids to the Country Club for the day and basically ignores him.

After several years of this, they find themselves in a marriage counselor's office discussing the topic of freedom. He complains about the Country Club bills she racks up with the kids on Saturdays.

Her face turns red and she almost shouts, "But I had to do something. I couldn't get you to get off the golf course and pay attention to your family. I have no freedom."

In turn, he looks at her with steely-blue and angry eyes and says, "You demand so much of me that I have to go play golf every weekend. That's the only way I can stay sane with all my traveling, your shopping habits, and the Country Club. I'm the one without freedom."

What is the problem here? Both the husband and wife don't understand the true definition of freedom. Let's examine the definition of freedom.

Freedom Defined

Used correctly, freedom works perfectly with love. Used incorrectly, it ignores love. Freedom can be defined or used in constructive or destructive ways.

Two definitions of freedom from Webster's Dictionary are shown below.

Freedom: Absence of necessity, coercion, or constraint in choice or action; independence; quality of being frank, open, or outspoken.

Free: Not subject to the control or domination of another; not determined by anything beyond its own nature or being; choosing or capable of choosing for itself.

The working definition we use in our GR8 Relationships is shown below.

Freedom is acting without force or manipulation or acting without controlling or being controlled.

You may think you are operating in freedom, making your own choices, but you may not be.

Look at the story above and think about the husband continuing to play golf every Saturday. Truly, he makes the choice to go play golf, but in the counseling session, what does he say? His wife's spending habits and lifestyle are compelling him to make that choice, as though he doesn't have control of it.

Look at the wife's response. "I had to go rack up the Country Club bill by taking the kids over there every Saturday." She contends that the husband was compelling her to make that choice since he would not stop playing golf every Saturday.

If you compare this scenario to the definition of Freedom we use in GR8 Relationships, you will likely note that both husband and wife were trying to manipulate the other person, not viewing freedom as a set of choices.

Realistically, he could choose to listen to his wife's needs and choose to play golf three times a month instead of every Saturday. She, on the other hand, could choose to hear that her spending habits put pressure on him financially. She has the freedom to spend less. Freedom is not about controlling or being controlled, it's about the reality of choices available to you.

Irresponsible Freedom

Unfortunately, freedom is more often used incorrectly. You are free to treat others improperly, manipulate and dominate them. As you likely noticed above, the *Flashing ME* was driving behavior. In fact, one of the greatest misuses of our freedom is when we fear *others will be irresponsible with their freedom.* That drives us to limit their freedom. Certainly, there is a proper place and time for that, as we will discuss later.

> *Of all tyrannies, a tyranny sincerely exercised for*
> *the good of its victims may be the most oppressive.*

C. S. Lewis

That profound statement is applicable for the individual, the family, and the government. Irresponsible freedom tends to see that I am free but does not believe I can be trusted to be free.

In the same chapter where God tells us that He sent His Son to die for us to set us free, He tells us to not use our freedom irresponsibly.

> *For you, brethren, have been called to liberty;*
> *only do not use liberty as an opportunity for the*
> *flesh, but through love serve one another.*

Galatians 5:13, NKJV

God urges us to be responsible, not irresponsible with our freedom. Focusing freedom on *ME*, flashing my *ME*, is irresponsible, please do not live that way!

*For this is the will of God, that by doing good you
may put to silence the ignorance of foolish men—
as free, yet not using liberty as a cloak for vice,
but as bondservants of God.*

1 Peter 2:15-16, NKJV

Freedom is often hard to accept, not as much for ourselves, as for others. When we push for maximum freedom for ourselves it tends to minimize the freedom for others.

Making wrong choices that go against God does not take away your adoption into God's family. However, wrong choices inhibit your spiritual growth, closeness with the Lord, and ultimately, eternal rewards. Yet you are still free to do just that! It is just being irresponsible with the freedom that God has provided.

Responsible and irresponsible freedom is the difference between what you are able to do and what you are encouraged and invited by God to do. It is the difference between can and will, between the possible and the beneficial. While freedom does give you the opportunity to sin, it is not condoning or licensing bad choices. Paul is emphatic about that.

*What shall we say then? Shall we continue in sin
that grace may abound? Certainly not! How shall
we who died to sin live any longer in it?*

Romans 6:1-2, NKJV

You are free to do whatever you want, but why would you? Once dead and now made alive in Christ, why would you want to walk as though you were still dead? That is why this verse points us back to the fundamental decision in life, which is: *will I depend on God or will I depend on something other than God?*

> *And do not present your members as instruments*
> *of unrighteousness to sin, but present yourselves*
> *to God as being alive from the dead, and your*
> *members as instruments of righteousness to God.*
> *For sin shall not have dominion over you, for you*
> *are not under law but under grace.*

Romans 6:13-14, NKJV

Forgiveness

The third F represents Forgiveness. In our GR8 Relationships programs, we have a working definition for Forgiveness. Forgiveness is a choice to lay the offense down, not mark or pay attention to where you laid it and never use it against them, not in your thoughts, speech, or action.

Forgiveness is a simple word and a simple action, but rarely understood. You need to understand what it really is and how to recognize weather you have actually done it.

Based on God's example with us, His Word, and my personal experience, I have learned that the best place to start for most relational problems is choosing to open and walk through the gates of forgiveness and confession. Forgiveness is so powerful, but vastly underused.

Forgiveness will heal a multitude of relationship problems, but it is not natural to consider it, especially shortly after someone has hurt you. The pain of what they did to you typically removes any thinking about forgiveness, which is your actual cure.

To take advantage of the power, you need to know the critical basics of forgiveness. This will require you to know the answers to two questions:

- What is a good working definition of forgiveness?
- How do you know if you have forgiven someone?

Applying the answers to those questions will help forgiveness become a part of your life. The more you know about forgiveness, the more you will likely use it, because better understanding can lead to better actions. Later in this book we give you the forgiveness process, and explain how to determine whether you have truly forgiven someone.

For life, clear definitions and clear thinking are imperative. That is true when relationships have problems, or someone has hurt you. Your feelings will often crowd out clear thinking and can lead you to bad actions that make the situation worse.

For many people *love* and *forgiveness* are not adequately defined or understood. You already have the definition for love, which is: *pursuing their best; patiently, kindly, sacrificially, and unconditionally*. If you love, you will forgive. But how?

Before we can answer this question, we need to understand another problem we encounter.

Guilt is the Problem

If forgiveness is the cure, guilt is the problem. And guess what? We are all guilty. That is why Jesus died for us. We all have been wronged, but worse, we all have hurt and sinned against others.

When guilt is present, several unhealthy strategies become active. For instance, when you are guilty, instead of confessing your guilt to the Lord and others, you may:

- Rationalize – "It really wasn't wrong! They deserved it!"
- Deny – "What's wrong with that? I didn't do anything wrong!"
- Scapegoat (blame) – "I wouldn't have done it if they . . ."

- Self-Punish (shame) – "I'll never be able to get over this. Why did I do something like that? How could I have been so dumb?"
- Medicate (alcohol, drugs) – "I don't want to think about it, I just want to feel better, now."
- Do Penance (good deeds) – "I'll make it up to them by . . ."
- Self-forgive – "I know that others, even God, have forgiven me, but I can't forgive myself."

All those strategies are flawed and will not provide healing. That last strategy, to self-forgive is a trap.

Consider the statement, "I know that others, even God, have forgiven me, but I can't forgive myself." What does that say about your view of other's and God's forgiveness? Worse yet, where does that put you regarding others and God?

See the problem? Others and God have forgiven you, but your opinion is their forgiveness was somehow ineffective, or they lied. Whatever the case, you do not agree that the offense is no longer an issue. You decide to hang onto it, because you have decided when forgiveness is or is not effective in your life.

Worse yet, you have placed yourself above the other people and God. But He states:

*If we confess our sins, He is faithful and just
to forgive our sins and cleanse us from all
unrighteousness.*

1 John 1:9, NKJV

The self-forgiveness strategy is not only flawed from putting yourself above others, but also from not understanding both real and false guilt in your life. Most likely you are suffering from false guilt.

On the other hand, when others are guilty, they have hurt you, so then you may try to use these strategies.

- Seek Revenge – Plot, try to, or get even.
- Carry Baggage – Drag the problem into other relationships.
- Draft Others – Enlist others to join the "cause" against the "jerk."
- Become a Victim – "Poor me." Everyone needs to rescue me.
- Hold grudges – Become bitter and resent the person.

Those strategies lead to a life of resentment, grudges, and bitterness, which is summed up in a great statement: "Bitterness is like drinking a bottle of poison and hoping the other person dies." Let's look at what Lewis Smedes says about forgiveness.

If we could only choose to forget the cruelest moments, we could, as time goes on, free ourselves from their pain. But the wrong sticks like a nettle in our memory. The only way to remove the nettle is with a surgical procedure called forgiveness. It is not as though forgiving were the remedy of choice among other options less effective but still useful. It is the only remedy. The remedy has existed since the first wrong done one human being by another. Yet, people still punish themselves with the pains of a past long gone. Or punish others in a futile passion to get revenge... Couples break their marriages and divide their families into weeping pieces. All because they will not make use of the means given to us for recovering from...insults and injuries.

Lewis Smedes, *The Art of Forgiving*[2]

Do you want the freedom of forgiveness, or the chains of unforgiveness?

<u>REFLECTIVE QUESTIONS</u>

1. What is your story regarding forgiveness? If there is someone you need to forgive, what is your plan to deal with that?

    _____

    _____

    _____

    _____

    _____

2. Is there something you are guilty about that you are using one of the strategies mentioned instead of confessing? Describe below.

    _____

    _____

    _____

    _____

    _____

3. Have others hurt you? If so, have you used inappropriate strategies listed above. Describe below.

    _____

    _____

_____

_____

_____

Confession

The fourth and final key, C, represents confession. Like feelings, freedom, and forgiveness, confession is an enormously powerful action once you understand it.

Confession is admitting you have done something wrong. Often that means others have been hurt. It does not matter who you are, in every relationship there are wrongs that need to be acknowledged and confessed. When you sin, God asks you to confess your sins to Him and to any others who are injured by your sins. Here's what we find in 1 John.

> *If we confess our sins, He is faithful and just to forgive us our sins and to cleanse us from all unrighteousness.*
>
> **1 John 1:9, NKJV**

Webster's Dictionary defines confession as follows: "To tell, to make known, to admit." The second part of the definition is: "To acknowledge a sin to God or to a priest." That is a good yet incomplete definition.

Consider the definition offered by Strong's Exhaustive Concordance: "To concede, not refuse, to promise, to not deny, or to admit and declare oneself guilty." That is a more Christian and complete definition. Why? Because the definition describes an action we may not want to take. Please understand and remember that in Christ we no longer need to defend ourselves, so it's okay to admit we did something wrong. Once you get this embedded into your heart and soul it will be easier to confess.

Here is the definition for confession we use at GR8 Relationships. *Confession is the external act from an internal change of heart.*

What I confess comes out of my mouth in words to God and reflects what is happening in my heart. My heart says, "I do not want to continue this type of behavior. I do not want to do that anymore." This definition of confession reflects the reality of physical laws. Two objects cannot occupy the same space at the same time. Consequently, if you have a change of heart, you must then expel the rebellious part of that heart that does not want to repent. It is both a spiritual and natural law of the universe. It is simply reality.

REFLECTIVE QUESTIONS

1. What confession do you need to make? Describe below.

    _____

    _____

    _____

    _____

    _____

2. How will the confession described above enhance your relationship with God? How will it enhance your relationship with others?

    _____

    _____

    _____

    _____

    _____

WHAT IS THE BEST ME?

Am I obeying God? Am I pursuing the best for others? The place to start for GR8 Relationships is to accept reality. Your *Best ME* accepts that it's not about ME. Your *Flashing ME* is the problem, and you are the only one who can refocus to pursue the best for others. When you understand that you are not a victim, you have choices, and you can control your thinking, feelings, and actions, then you give your relationships the best chance to be great.

It is so easy to find fault in others and focus on how you wish they would change. Of course it is. But the fact is you can only control your behavior. You can contain your *Flashing ME* only by the power of the Holy Spirit who provides you the ability to use the four relationship tools: Feelings, Freedom, Forgiveness and Confession.

Other tools, assessments, and professional counseling can be beneficial, but too often they reinforce the problem: getting you to think too much about yourself. The better approach is to use the 3 Fs and a C to find ways to pursue the best for others.

Let's explore how to make the most of Feelings, Freedom, Forgiveness and Confession in a way that supports your growth and supports relationships.

Feelings

Feelings are best used when we recognize that they are a *response* to something and *untrustworthy*, as we mentioned earlier. Once you learn and apply the following two statements, you can see dramatic change.

1) Feelings are primarily responders, and

2) Feelings are often untrustworthy.

The best way to make feelings work for you is to put them in the context of Think-Feel-Act or Think-Act-Feel. With that in mind, consider the following scripture passage.

> *Jesus said to him, "you shall love the Lord your God with all your heart, with all your soul, and with all your mind." This is the first and great commandment. And the second is like it: "You shall love your neighbor as yourself." On these two commandments hang all the Law and the Prophets.*

Matthew 22:37-40, NJKV

Which is first in those verses – Thinking, Feeling, or Acting?

Everything depends on what *love* is. Most people would say that *love* is a feeling, so, the conclusion would be that God is asking you to act on a feeling. However, the construction of the sentence indicates that *love* is a verb; therefore, an action occurs first. God is asking you to decide. Here is a working definition of love: *Pursuing their best; patiently, kindly, sacrificially, and unconditionally.* This definition shows that love is a decision! A decision requires thinking to make a conscious choice. Possibly more importantly, you read the scripture, or have it told to you first. You think and process the information first, even if you decide that love *is* a feeling. So, a reasonable conclusion is that *thinking* is first in those verses.

Act the Way You Want to Feel

Research shows that if you feel depressed, acting differently than your feelings will impact how you feel. In fact, consider the following:

> *If you extend your soul to the hungry and satisfy the afflicted soul, then your light shall dawn in the darkness, and your darkness shall be as the noonday.*

Isaiah 58:10, NKJV

When you serve others, your darkness is turned to light, because you are no longer focused on yourself. God wants you to serve others which models His behavior instead of flashing your *Me*.

You can experiment on yourself with a simple technique to prove that actions can alter feelings. Try it the next time you are feeling sad.

Use this three-step process with your face, body and breathing or speech. Start with your face.

Just ask yourself, "How would I like to feel right now?" If you answer happy, joyful, or peaceful, put a smile or pleasant expression on your face. (Even if you answered sad you can still try this.)

Next, look at your body. Are your shoulders slumped, head down? Are you moving slowly? Change your body to a position that reflects the word you chose. At minimum, sit or stand up straight, shoulders back, chin up and good posture. Start moving with a little more energy.

Finally, think about your breathing and speech. Take some deep breaths, and if you need to speak, do so with energy and articulation. You will soon see the critical element that makes this technique work.

If you do those three steps, you put your body out of sync with your emotions. When your emotions are sad but your body is happy, researchers call this dissonance, meaning emotions and actions are not equal.

You have two options: change your emotions to be like your body or change your body to be like your emotions. If you decide to let your body remain happy you will see that emotions are responding to your actions. Not only are they responding to your actions, but more importantly responding to your thinking, which is driving your actions.

You might say, "But that is just being fake!"

That could be the case, but if you decide happy or joyful is more important to you than being sad, it is not fake. Instead, you are acting true to your values or priorities. Being depressed is not what you value, which is the real fake item. This technique can help you to be real.

Changing your feelings through action is somewhat like repairing something that is broken. The broken pieces need to be realigned and reconnected to be restored.

Recently, I needed to repair a wooden chair. Since people would be using the chair, the repair needed to be done correctly, so the chair would not break when someone sat in it. I aligned the broken pieces, applied glue, clamped the pieces together then waited for 24 hours based on the directions on the glue.

After some drying time for the glue, I removed the clamp. The two broken pieces were now reconnected and, because they were properly realigned, the chair was restored to its intended usefulness.

Using that example, actions are like the glue while feelings are like the broken pieces. Thinking is the clamp that keeps the pieces aligned while the glue hardens. Consider using actions to help you or others make some changes to feelings.

Help Attitudes Change

Acting the way you want to feel, as described above, can also work on attitudes. Behavior can be easier to change than an attitude or feeling because it is tangible. If you act consistently, despite your feelings, then feelings will eventually respond.

Suppose you have a friend that has a bad attitude about another person.

You could say something like this. "You've stated that you don't like Joe. Since you are around him a lot, it would be best to find a way to make the relationship work better than it is now."

"Since I know that you value kindness, would you be willing to do a small experiment for the next month? You don't need to become his friend, but would you be willing to smile and offer a pleasant greeting each time you see him during the next month?"

If they say no, you could ask them what they would be willing to do to demonstrate kindness, which you know is one of their values. Then ask if they would be willing to take that action.

This is not a time to try to convince them to be better person, shame them into change or make them do anything. You are only calling them to act on their values. When people freely act on their own values, they will have more energy to act. And, you can offer to be an accountability partner, which is often a great help.

People who are willing to take that type of action for at least 30 days will see themselves change, even if the other person does not.

Thinking/Feeling Principle

Which is easiest to change – thinking or acting? Acting is often chosen and written about, but thinking is actually easier to change.

Consider this: thinking about changing our actions precedes the actions, right? That does not mean that you believe the thinking, but you are acting on it nevertheless.

The more you act consistently with your thinking the more it will be reinforced, impacting your beliefs and your feelings. You can simplify your life when you consider the power of thinking. If you think correctly, it will drive good actions and at some point, good feelings. Unfortunately, if your thinking is bad, it will drive incorrect actions and feelings. So, what you are thinking is especially important!

In fact, the most important thing in your life is your thinking because it drives everything else that you do or feel. What you think about is what your life reflects in your actions and feelings. And consider this: If you're thinking about God does not match God's Word, then your thinking is distorted, impacting all areas of your life.

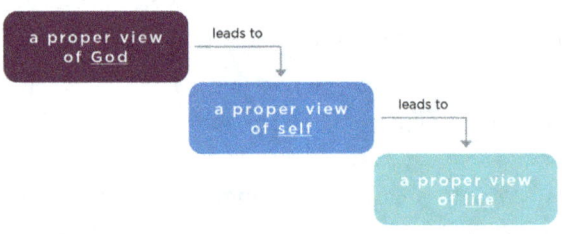

The graphic shows how important it is to have a proper view of God. It was adapted from Jim Berg in his book *Changed Into His Image*.[3] Your thinking is either based on truth or lies. If truth, you have a much better chance to understand how life works. If lies, you are confused, trying to control everything to make you happy.

A Transformation System

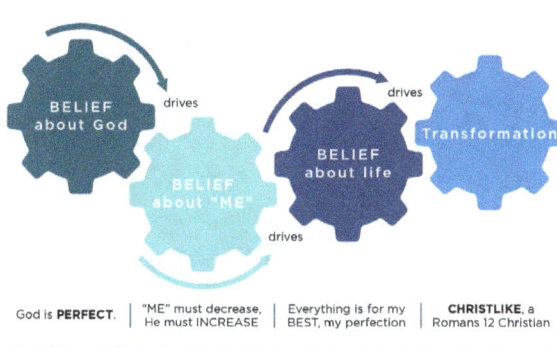

| God is **PERFECT**. | "ME" must decrease, He must INCREASE | Everything is for my BEST, my perfection | **CHRISTLIKE**, a Romans 12 Christian |

God is **perfect**. I am **perfect** and invited to **be perfected**.

That idea has been expanded into our transformation system, which is part of the coming book, *What Are You Thinking?!?!*

> *The mind governed by the flesh is death, but the mind governed by the Spirit is life and peace.*

Romans 8:6, NIV

The scripture above indicates that thinking drives you in the direction of life or death. Using life or death shows how critical your thinking is and what is going on in your mind is so important as we see in many scriptures.

Your thinking is the only thing you can control. Since thinking leads to your actions, you will be able to control your actions. You can control your attitude and how you see life because you're thinking about those things creates the attitude and perception. How you think about things is what becomes your attitude and perspective on life.

> *For the weapons of our warfare are not carnal*
> *but mighty in God for pulling down strongholds,*
> *casting down arguments and every high thing*
> *that exalts itself against the knowledge of God,*
> *bringing every thought into captivity to the*
> *obedience of Christ*

2 Corinthians 10:4-5, NKJV

Notice the words "bringing every thought into captivity . . ." That is a clear statement that you can control your thoughts. You may not be able to prevent thoughts from entering your mind, but you can control whether they stay, especially through the power of Christ.

The entirety of God's Word is about changing your thinking to the reality of God's truth. That is why the Bible constantly refers to the mind. Even those passages that refer to the heart are almost always referring to the *essence of who you are,* which is aimed at your thinking.

The following are two great scripture passages about thinking.

I beseech you therefore, brethren, by the mercies of God, that you present your bodies a living sacrifice, holy, acceptable to God, which is your reasonable service. And do not be conformed to this world, but be transformed by the renewing of your mind, that you may prove what is that good and acceptable and perfect will of God.

Romans 12:1-2, NKJV

Finally, brethren, whatever things are true, whatever things are noble, whatever things are just, whatever things are pure, whatever things are lovely, whatever things are of good report, if there is any virtue and if there is anything praiseworthy—meditate on these things.

Philippians 4:8, NKJV

Build a solid foundation of good thinking and good values based on scripture, then, act based on that foundation and eventually your feelings will respond.

In addition, choose the power of the Holy Spirit to guide your thinking, so that your sin nature, which is wired into self-seeking thoughts, will not introduce fear, uncertainty, and doubt. As the scriptures above note, *renew your mind* and *meditate on what is just, pure, lovely and of good report.* Put your thinking in the right place, aligned with God's Word, which will lead your actions and feelings down a constructive path.

Freedom

As simple as it sounds, freedom used correctly in a relationship is a powerful way to live. By accepting the reality of choices, instead of reacting to situations, you begin to see how much self-control or self-governance you have in your life. When you are self-governing, you accept that other people have choices, too. If you forget or ignore their freedom, you may try to force or manipulate others to choose what you want.

As mentioned earlier, freedom is one of the most crucial principles for any relationship,

Used correctly, it works perfectly when placed underneath love. If not underneath love, freedom is often irresponsible.

Freedom – Great for Relationships

When freedom is applied to relationships it emphasizes the critical truth that everyone has the ability to make their own choices. Everyone is responsible for their own decisions. When you have freedom in a relationship, you are not being controlled by the other person. And the other person is free to make, and be responsible for, their own choices. It would be a strange argument to think a relationship would work better by using manipulation and control instead of freedom and responsibility.

Responsible Freedom

As a Christian you have enormous freedom through the saving grace of Christ.

Our glorious Savior, Jesus Christ, gave His children victory over the bondage of our sin nature. You have the liberty to choose right actions lead by His power and grace. Christ clearly died for us to free you.

> *Stand fast therefore in the liberty by which Christ has made us free, and do not be entangled again with a yoke of bondage.*

> **Galatians 5:1, NKJV**

What a great verse. You were saved for freedom. And used correctly, freedom helps you see others differently, and change your focus on others as well as yourself.

When you are responsible with your freedom, your outward focus changes so you see the abilities, rights, and choices that others have. You don't have to like or even put up with others' choices, but you know they can choose whatever they want. Whatever their choice, good or bad, you are not driven or feel responsible to make them change.

Instead of treating people as machines with buttons to manipulate, you respect them as free moral agents who have the freedom to choose and the responsibility for their own decisions. It is God's job to change them, not yours. You can participate with God in helping them change, but you are not taking on the role of the Junior Holy Spirit in their life.

Additionally, responsible freedom impacts your inward focus, internal thoughts and behavior. You will see clearly how many options and choices you have rather than thinking you are powerless over your life, circumstances, and people around you. In fact, you will encourage, trust, and accept your own freedom to make choices. Living in freedom, you refuse to be manipulated or dominated by your circumstances, and choose a life based on your values.

Hopefully those values are rooted in truth, and you can find your pleasure in doing right yourself, rather than forcing others to do it.

Freedom Is Divine

God is *the* model for freedom in relationships. God is the only one who has complete control and sovereignty. He is all powerful, and everything that happens is part of His infinitely good plan.

> *The lot is cast into the lap, but its every decision is from the LORD.*

> **Proverbs 16:33, NKJV**

> *A man's heart plans his way, but the LORD directs his steps.*

> **Proverbs 16:9, NKJV**

> *Who has ascended into heaven, or descended? Who has gathered the wind in His fists? Who has bound the waters in a garment? Who has established all the ends of the earth? What is His name, and what is His Son's name, if you know?*

> **Proverbs 30:4, NKJV**

We have limited power, even over our own lives, yet we spend time trying to manipulate or dominate others in order to get what we want. Notice the irony. God allows freedom, but we try to control, manipulate or dominate. God can control but does not; we cannot control but tirelessly try to do so.

God does not force us to do what is right. He does not make us glorify Him, even though He deserves all glory. He does not act as a tyrant giving ultimatums.

He invites, offers a better way, gives energy through His Holy Spirit to live that better way, then allows us to ignore what is right and mess up if we choose!

REFLECTIVE QUESTIONS
– FREEDOM

- Think of a recent situation where you felt you didn't have the freedom to make your own choices. Briefly describe the situation, then list the choices you had in the situation. How would making a different choice, changed the outcome?

_____

_____

_____

_____

_____

_____

- What new concept did you learn about freedom in this section of content?

_____

_____

_____

_____

_____

_____

- Describe a relationship in your life where you can recognize and apply the freedom Christ has given you?

  Stand fast therefore in the liberty by which Christ has made us free, and do not be entangled again with a yoke of bondage.

  Galatians 5:1, NKJV

  _____

  _____

  _____

  _____

  _____

  _____

Forgiveness

Forgiveness is a powerful tool in life and relationships, and has many benefits. First of all, forgiveness benefits the forgiver more than anyone. Some key benefits of forgiveness are described below.

Forgiveness Pleases God

And be kind to one another, tenderhearted, forgiving one another, just as God in Christ also forgave you.

Ephesians 4:32, NKJV

Does the verse give any options to not forgive? Do you forgive if the other person has met some specific criteria? No. We have only an example to follow: God. We did not deserve it, yet He asked Christ to pay the penalty for our sin and Christ agreed.

Forgiving others is like thanking God for forgiving you. When you tame your *Flashing ME*, you can clearly see the boundless mercy God has shown you. So: forgiving is obeying God, which pleases Him.

Forgiveness Imitates God

Forgiveness is truly a divine action. When you forgive you imitate what God would do. Without the example and grace of God, how many would ever choose to forgive others? Looking at my life, without trusting in God's justice and omniscience, I am not sure how much forgiveness would be there.

Forgiveness not only thanks God, but it also confirms that you want to act like God, not like your sin nature. It says that you trust what He says and what He has done. And you want to imitate His amazing example.

Forgiveness Escapes Serious Consequences

The above reasons are enough, but you may not see them as that important.

Why, because it is natural to be asking something like, "Okay, but what's in it for *ME*?" Ironically, whether self-control or self-absorption is your goal, forgiveness is the *best* option either way. You may be doing it for self-control, because the Lord asked you to follow His example, so you are a godly example to the world. Or you may be doing it for self-absorption, because you want to get out of the pain and move on. Either way, there is a huge benefit, because you escape the trap of an unforgiving, bitter heart.

Your Choice

You can choose to be controlled by the past or by God, controlled by the sins that were done to you or forgive and trust that the Lord will take care of it. It is your choice.

Clearly, God wants you to forgive. But is that a command or a choice? Do you forgive because you are commanded to do so? When you feel obligated or required to do something, even if it is 100 percent right, you may tend to ignore it, complain about having to do it, or worse yet, rebel and do the opposite.

God wants you to live in freedom, not bondage. Forgiveness releases you from the bondage of bitterness and vengeance. A commandment to forgive obviously does not make it happen. Ultimately you choose forgiveness based on an internal act of the will.

God seems to be saying, "Forgiveness is the best way to deal with your memory of wrongful pain. It is an opportunity to be free of the pain and probably help other people, even the person who hurt you. It is your choice to trust My way or yours. And by the way, the alternative to forgiving, bitterness and vengeance, only makes the pain last longer. It will affect you emotionally, mentally, and physically, and even generations to come. Please, don't choose that."

Forgiveness puts a new future before you and gives you a new way to see those who hurt you. It may be the one act that allows you to truly imitate God, the original, Master Forgiver.

Forgiveness Process

Forgiveness is like treating a wound. Any wrong done toward you is like a physical wound to your body. It may be just a bruise, or worse yet, a deep cut. If untreated you will lose blood, risk infection and may even die if the cut is bad. If you were physically cut, the basic medical steps to follow are listed below.

1. *Stop the bleeding*: Apply gentle pressure with a clean cloth or bandage. If bleeding persists, seek emergency assistance.
2. *Clean the wound*: Rinse the wound well with clear water. Thorough wound cleaning reduces the risk of tetanus. Use soap and a washcloth to clean the area around the wound.
3. *Apply an antibiotic*: After you clean the wound, apply a thin layer of an antibiotic cream or ointment to discourage infection and help your body close the wound.
4. *Cover the wound*: Bandages can help keep the wound clean and keep harmful bacteria out.
5. *Change the dressing regularly*: Do so at least daily or whenever it becomes wet or dirty.
6. *Watch for signs of infection*: See your doctor if the wound does not heal or if you notice any redness, drainage or swelling.
7. Enjoy healing.

Just like a physical wound, the wrong done to you needs treatment, a step-by-step process. Whatever they did to you, whatever the wrong, it is painful and needs treatment. When you follow a straightforward process, you can more easily understand forgiveness. It can help you understand the *how* of forgiveness taking something abstract and making it concrete. Look at the medical steps and the spiritual steps side-by-side.

medical	spiritual
STEP ONE: Stop the bleeding	Face your humanity
STEP TWO: Clean the wound	Overlook revenge
STEP THREE: Apply antibiotic	Renew your mind
STEP FOUR: Cover the wound	Give it up, grasp it no more
STEP FIVE: Change the dressing regularly	Apply your decision
STEP SIX: Look for signs of infection	Validate and verify your decision
STEP SEVEN: Enjoy healing	Enjoy healing and freedom

Step One: Stop the Bleeding – Face Your Humanity

This step does not release the other person from accountability for what they did. At this stage, you do not have to believe that they will once again be a close friend, trustworthy spouse or incapable of doing the same harm to us again. But you can choose to take them back into your imperfect world. That scoundrel, your enemy, is a faulty, bruised, imperfect human, just like you are. They are still blamable and accountable for the wrong done, but for the grace of God there go you and me.

A Great Example

Yehiel Dinur was a witness during the trial of Adolf Eichmann. Dinur entered the courtroom and stared at the man behind the bulletproof glass—the man who had presided over the slaughter of millions. The court was hushed as a victim confronted a butcher.

Then suddenly Dinur began to sob and collapsed to the floor. As he explained later in an interview, what struck him at that instant was a terrifying realization. "I saw that I am capable to do this . . . Exactly like he."

The reporter interviewing Dinur asked, "How was it possible for a man to act as Eichmann acted? Was he a monster? A madman? Or was he perhaps something even more terrifying…Was he normal?"

Yehiel Dinur, in a moment of chilling clarity said, "Eichmann is in all of us."

That is what this first step is about. See whoever wronged you as a person, faulty just like you are. When we see the humanity of the person who wronged us, the bleeding is under control.

Step Two: Clean the Wound – Overlook Revenge

Overlook your *assumed* right to revenge or to get even. We think we have the right to revenge, but we do not. Revenge is God's right alone.

*Repay no one evil for evil. Have regard for good
things in the sight of all men. If it is possible,
as much as depends on you, live peaceably with
all men. Beloved, do not avenge yourselves, but
rather give place to wrath; for it is written,
"Vengeance is Mine, I will repay," says the Lord.*

Romans 12:17-19, NKJV

Forgiveness accepts God's justice and rejects our idea of justice. When we assume the role of avenger, we are trying to be God. We say we want justice, but if we are honest with ourselves, we know we may want to do just a bit more to them than they did to us. When we try to get even we multiply our sin, toward the other person and toward God by demanding He get off His throne so we can take charge.

Vengeance grows in the soil of pride. It is a right we never had, a lie that Satan wants us to believe. But forgiveness gives up the sinful desire for vengeance. Forgiveness provides healing, a brighter future, and hope.

*bearing with one another, and forgiving one
another, if anyone has a complaint against
another; even as Christ forgave you, so you also
must do.*

Colossians 3:13, NKJV

You are drawing a line in the sand, handing vengeance to God, and moving forward. You are letting God clean the wound.

Step Three: Apply Antibiotic – Renew Your Mind

Before you entered the first step of forgiveness, your feelings toward the offender may have been hate, bitterness, and anger. You wanted bad things to happen to the person who did bad things to you. That is what hate is all about. Since feelings are primarily responders, thinking and actions need to change to revise your feelings. Remember the order: first think, then act or feel.

Choose to believe truth like you find in Romans.

And we know that all things work together for good to those who love God, to those who are the called according to His purpose.

Romans 8:28, NKJV

We have trivialized and misused this verse greatly, but it is still true and applicable. God fully understands your situation. It has not caught Him off guard.

Choose to see the offender as an instrument of God. Remember that God is using that person to develop and shape you to be more like Jesus Christ. That may be a hard pill to swallow, but if we do not swallow, we're not trusting God. Further, we miss out on blessings that can only come from trusting God through forgiveness.

When we meditate on truth, we may feel a real (perhaps reluctant) wish that some good things might come to the offender. The feeling of good may be hesitant at the start, but it will be there as we meditate on truth and as God changes our thinking. We may backslide along the way but persevering with truth creates the framework for our feelings to respond. Apply the Antibiotic of Truth, and healing will begin.

You can renew your mind to God's truth and see the beauty of forgiveness but what is forgiveness? What are doing when you forgive?

If you do not have a definition of a word, how can you know it is being used correctly? When God said that He forgave you when you placed your trust in Jesus' death, burial, and resurrection, what did He do? If you can answer that you are on the right path.

Just like love needs a clear, biblical definition, so does forgiveness. When you forgive someone, you decide to never use that offense against them or pay attention to it again. Think about that! You unhand the *weapon* that could be used on them. You give it up, stop grasping, stop holding onto the offense.

So, here is our working definition: Forgiveness is a choice to lay the offense down, not mark or pay attention to where you laid it and never use it against them, not in your thoughts, speech, or action.

And here is a shorter version to memorize: Never abusing them for the wrong they did to you, not in thought, word, or action.

Step Four: Cover the Wound -- Give it Up, Grasp it No More

In this step you make the following decisions.
- You decide, conclude, commit to – stop holding onto the offense.
- You decide, conclude, commit to – never use the offense against them again, to never pay attention to it again.
- You decide, conclude, commit to – unhand the "weapon" you could use against them.
- You decide, conclude, commit to – move forward rather than remain stuck in the past.
- You decide, conclude, commit to – bless them and free yourself.
- You decide, conclude, commit to *forgive.*

Bitterness keeps you stuck in the past, but forgiveness allows you to move forward into the future. This does not mean you need to forgive and forget, as some people say. Forgetting is not required for forgiveness, though sometimes it comes afterward.

Some people think God forgives and forgets based on this verse from Jeremiah.

> . . . *For I will forgive their iniquity, and their sin I will remember no more.*

Jeremiah 31:34, NKJV

If God forgives this way, shouldn't we? Absolutely. According to Strong's dictionary, "remember" means "to mark (to be recognized), or it implies "to mention".

When God is challenged to 'remember' the meaning is better taken as 'pay attention to' since nothing ever escapes God's omniscience (Psalms 89:47). God does not forget the way we do. He does not pay attention to or mark our sin against us, because He sees us through the blood of Jesus. We are accepted, because of Jesus' death, burial, and resurrection. Now our sins are no longer a barrier between God and us. Thank God for that! We know from this that when God forgives us, He does not use our sin against us ever again.

For example, suppose you are reading a book and you want to remember a statement in it. You could memorize it, but more likely you use a highlighter pen, underline it, use a sticky note, and fold the page to mark the place so your attention will be drawn to it.

God the Father will not do that. He has decided not to pay attention to what the Son has covered. God has moved into a different relationship with us.

How about letting it go? God knows what is best for you and this situation. How about not marking it against them? Why keep hurting yourself?

> *A rattlesnake, if cornered, will become so angry it will bite itself. That is exactly what the harboring of hate and resentment against others is – a biting of oneself. We think we are harming others in holding these spites and hates, but the deeper harm is to ourselves.*

E. Stanley Jones

It is time to give it up so that you can cover the wound and allow it to heal.

Step Five: Change the Dressing Regularly – Apply Your Decision

Consider the scars on your body. They are memorials to healing.

I have some significant scars on my body from a skiing accident and near-death experience, as well as two back operations. Those situations were extremely painful at the time but they are not painful now because they are healed.

If I had some bad thinking, I could look at those scars, remember the pain, and put myself back into the pain and difficulty of each situation. But why would I do that? Those situations are over, and the scars are proof of the healing. Wouldn't it be better to see the scars and remember the fact the situation is over, and I am healed?

That is why we in our GR8 Relationships program believe in *Forgive and Remember.* Once you have experienced the power of forgiveness, you will have multiple scars, all healed, rather than open wounds.

Forgive and remember helps for old and new wounds. When you remember or reflect on any old wound, then you can remember that it is now a scar, a healed wound, and there is no need to reopen it. When you have a new wound, you can remember the scars and healing from the old wounds. That will help you consider forgiving again.

Without forgiveness you leave wounds open, and they turn into bloody messes. That's not what God wants for you!

Once you have forgiven do whatever you can do to remember the forgiveness, because in the heat of emotion it is easy to forget. When you make the decision to forgive in Step Four, you commit to new thinking: no longer seeking revenge, but letting it go instead. Memorialize that thinking with an action and a date. Think of this step like baptism. Baptism does not save us, but is a testimony, a memorial to the most important decision you and I will ever make; to trust God for our eternity.

Step Six: Look for Signs of Infection – Validate and Verify Your Decision

You will have opportunities to move backward toward vengeance and bitterness – the next time you get into an argument, feel slighted, or see, hear, smell, taste, or touch something that reminds you of what happened. Anytime you start Flashing your *ME* with them is a time you may move back toward bitterness.

So, how do you deal with these thoughts about what they did to you? You say you forgave, but the thoughts keep coming up. It depends on the answer to one critical question. Before you ask the critical question, consider these options:

- Option One: You did not forgive when you said you did.
- Option Two: You did forgive and need to forgive again.
- Option Three: You did forgive and need to validate your forgiveness.

And the simple question is, "Did I forgive them when I said I did?"

The answer to the question is either yes or no. Maybe means no because there will be no freedom.

Forgiveness is about freeing you from the bondage of their offense to you.

Right now, ask that question about the wrong the person did to you. "Did I forgive them when I said I did?" Yes or No?

If your answer is no, that's option one above. Ask the Lord to help you understand forgiveness and prepare you to forgive. Go back to Step one and start the forgiveness process from the beginning.

But your answer could be yes, you know that you forgave, you remember the date and used the application tool. But perhaps you let your bad thinking control you, resulting in just wanting revenge for doing *that* to you. That is option two above. You are paying attention to or have marked the location of the weapon and have started using it again. The solution: go back to step one and forgive again.

Finally, your answer is yes, but you continue to have thoughts about what happened. Your thoughts are not revengeful or bitter; you just remember the pain of going through that event. Instead of going back to step one, do these three things:

1. Use the power of 2 Corinthians 10:4-5. At the end of verse 5 it says, "bringing every thought into captivity to the obedience of Christ."

2. Hand the thoughts to Jesus Christ, saying, "Lord, I know that I forgave, that I didn't lie about the

forgiveness, and You know I did not lie. You deal with the thoughts and remove them from me."

3. Move quickly to step seven.

As you continue to subject those thoughts to Christ, you will struggle with them less, and the wound will heal.

Step Seven: Enjoy Healing – and Freedom

If you have not forgiven, it will be extremely hard to do what this step requires. If you have forgiven, this step speeds the healing.

Louie had a severe break in her left arm at the elbow that required a metal plate and screws to give her use of the arm again. Not long after the surgery, the doctor prescribed working with a physical therapist to rebuild the muscles and maximize the flexibility of her elbow. That therapy was not fun, it was painful, but it was necessary in order to maximize the healing and use of her arm.

Step seven is like working with a therapist. What you are asked to do may not be easy, but it is imperative if you want freedom and healing. Here is what this step requires:

- Praying for God's blessing upon them.
- Encouraging them.
- Pursue their best by finding ways to serve them.

When you come through step six and verify that you have forgiven, this step will help you continue to move forward. Without this last step it will be easy to let the memory of the pain of what they did to you pull you back toward vengeance and bitterness. There is immense power in this step.

You might be saying, "You have got to be kidding! You are asking me to not only let the offense go, but now you are asking me to pray blessing upon them!"

Yes, I am because it is what Christ did. This step is following the marvelous example of Jesus Christ.

We participated with the people of Jerusalem in the crucifixion of Jesus. He was beaten and tortured then hung on the cross. As Jesus was on the cross, He asked His Father to forgive us and the people of Jerusalem. He then died, rose again, and appeared to many people. Then He did something we want to imitate.

> *And being assembled together with them, He commanded them not to depart from Jerusalem, but to wait for the Promise of the Father, "which," He said, "you have heard from Me.*
>
> *But you shall receive power when the Holy Spirit has come upon you; and you shall be witnesses to Me in Jerusalem, and in all Judea and Samaria, and to the end of the earth.*

Acts 1:4, 8, NKJV

Jesus sent the Holy Spirit to the disciples to bless Jerusalem, the very people who did Him wrong! Blessing people who have harmed you is impossible without forgiveness. Until you, too, forgive those who have wronged you, you cannot pray God's blessing upon them, encourage them, or pursue their best. And until you do that you will not experience the freedom and healing God wants for you.

Ensure the healing. Pray for them, bless them, and find ways to pursue their best. Enjoy the freedom.

Confession Process

In my experience confession is a significant factor in maintaining the longevity of a relationship and as important as forgiveness.

Before thinking about how to confess it is critical to define what you are doing. What is confession?

Confession is an external act of an internal change of heart

Additionally, the order of confession is critical: first to God, then to others.

As you saw with forgiveness, a process or steps can help make something abstract more concrete and applicable. So, confession can also be arranged into steps.

Step One: Choose Humility

Humility is essential for confession. Without it you remain defensive and judgmental and unable to see the real issues that are going on in your life. The prideful person is always less available to receive because he or she does not believe she needs to receive. The humble person is in the proper posture to receive something good.

More importantly, when you are humble you make yourself available to receive God's grace.

*Likewise you younger people, submit yourselves
to your elders. Yes, all of you be submissive to
one another, and be clothed with humility, for
"God resists the proud, but gives grace to the
humble." Therefore humble yourselves under the
mighty hand of God, that He may exalt you in
due time, casting all your care upon Him, for
He cares for you.*

1 Peter 5:5-7, NKJV

Step Two: Own Your Guilt. Do Not Excuse It.

One of the more difficult things for you to do
in life is own what you have done and accept the
consequences. The temptation to pass the buck and
blame someone else is strong. But excuses are empty.

As actor Steven Grayhm said, "Excuses are the tools
with which a person with no purpose in view builds for
themselves great monuments of nothing."

Consider a few of the common excuses used. Ask
yourself whether the excuse holds up in light of the
reply.

excuse	answer	excuse	answer
It happened a long time ago	Why are you thinking about it?	They will not understand	Irrelevant, do the right thing
They have moved away	They can be found	I will do it later	Later never comes
It was such a small offense	It still can create major damage	I will only do it again	And you can confess again.
Things are better	Good, resolve it now	They were more wrong	This is about you, not them
I am just being too sensitive	Be more sensitive because they may be sensitive too	If I purpose not to do it again, won't that be enough?	That does not deal with this sin. Confess to remove its power
No one's perfect	That is not the issue, sin is the issue	If I do, it will get my friends in trouble	You do not have to involve them, confess about you

Step Three: Name the Real Offense

Confession requires honesty, objectivity, and reality. It is about what is going on. This is not something you can do on your own power. Left to your own devices you will "chicken out" and talk about petty issues or peripheral sin. To really get to the issue you ask God to reveal the real hurt, the real wrong, the real offense.

Bill Gothard, a minister, writer, and the founder of the Institute in Basic Life Principles suggests, "It is relatively easy to remember the faults of others, but when it comes to listing our own faults, we may discover a lapse of memory."

That is why you desperately need the wisdom of the Psalmist who writes,

Search, me, O God, and know my heart; Try me, and know my anxieties; And see if there is any wicked way in me and lead me in the way everlasting.

Psalm 139: 23-24, NKJV

Ask God to show you the real offense and then be willing to explicitly name each one of them. I suggest making a written list.

Step Four: Feel the Offense as they Felt It

Empathy involves attempting to see life from another's person's perspective, understanding their pain, and then doing something about that pain. When it comes to confession you may feel that you are only 10 percent wrong while the other person feels you are the one who is 100 percent wrong.

It is often the case that you think something is no big deal, but another person considers it to be a huge deal. You do not have to necessarily understand another person's pain, but you do need to at least attempt to see it through their eyes. Be willing to grasp another's pain to a degree that you are moved to do something about relieving the pain, like confessing if you were the one that created the pain.

Step Five: Earnestly Repent of your Sin

When you repent you align your heart with God, which is what God wants. He wants an intimate relationship with you that requires hearts aligning. The outcome of repentance is fantastic, but the process is not always fun because it requires remorse for your sin.

(And just in case you did not know, repentance is an internal change of heart and mind, and exactly what you do to experience genuine joy in the forgiveness of God. Simply put, repentance involves a 180 degree turn from sin and turn toward doing what is right.)

Faking repentance means you want others to tolerate your sin without changing. It is like saying, "I am just that way, put up with it."

Step Six: Soberly Confess your Sin

As you have already read, confession first takes place with God and then with the other person you have wronged and injured. Do not forget that ***confession is the external act of the internal change of heart***. So confession, while centered on an internal change, involves external action. You ask for forgiveness from God and, when appropriate, ask others too.

> *If we confess our sins, He is faithful and just to forgive us our sins and to cleanse us from all unrighteousness.*
>
> **1 John 1:9, NKJV**

Step Seven: Sincerely Thank God for the Conflict

Thank the Lord for the conflict. Most people avoid conflict like the plague. It should not be so among believers. Conflict is actually a great time for learning and development. More importantly, God can bless us immensely even if the conflict was evil. Remember how Joseph was severely mistreated by his brothers, yet he said,

> *. . . you meant evil against me, but God meant it for good. . . And St. Paul clearly tells us God is at work in all, even the worst, situations.*

Genesis 50:20, NKJV

> *And we know that all things work together for good to those who love God, to those who are the called according to His purpose.*

Romans 8:28, NKJV

Give thanks to God in all things because He alone knows how sin will be used for His good purposes. He alone is in control of all things. And He alone can make something good out of something sinful.

If you are now ready to deal honestly with the real guilt in your life, please sincerely consider praying this prayer.

> *Lord Jesus, I want to thank You for loving me and accepting me. I want to confess any sin in my life right now . . . and by faith I claim Your forgiveness as mine for eternity.*

Please help me to never become insensitive to the moving of Your convicting hand. I pray that You will take me and grow me up and make me like You, so my life will reflect Your unconditional love and grace, Amen.

The scriptures listed below will reinforce how God will build you up, because He is dedicated to you, desiring the best for you.

- Psalm 27:5-6
- Psalm 27:11-14
- Isaiah 41:10-11
- Isaiah 42:6
- Lamentations 3:22
- Habakkuk 3:17-19
- Matthew 11:28
- John 16:33
- Romans 8:37-39
- Ephesians 5:20
- 1 Peter 1:3-9

EPILOGUE

Years ago, Louie and I found ourselves in a heart-breaking situation in our marriage, and by the grace of God our lives were transformed through the help of Dr. Marlin Howe, a skilled, funny, and gracious pastor and counsellor. We have learned a lot about ourselves, each other, and the simplicity of the problem and the solution. We were so grateful to have had people who could come alongside us and help us through that we founded the *GR8 Relationships* program to teach others the simple truth of relationships done God's way. That means not only like He says, but also like He does. This is our way to sow into others the amazing guidance, help and restoration God has given us for our marriage.

Relationships start with two people trying to navigate life. Two human beings living in harmony is impossible without God's truth. We have found through our years of counseling couples that they seldom understand how to love and care for each other. In fact, they often say they love each other, and in their next sentence speak vile thoughts about each other. Why? The *Flashing ME* damages a relationship as each person tries desperately to make sure their wants and needs are addressed. When couples learn to turn their focus away from ME and pursue the best for their spouse; patiently, kindly, sacrificially, and unconditionally, the relationship or marriage can blossom.

The problem and the solution are the foundation. The four tools help rebuild the marriage on it. It is easier to remember the tools with *Three F's and a C.* These letters represent Feelings, Freedom, Forgiveness and Confession. Of the four we have found that the underpinning of Forgiveness and Confession drives the success of couples working through any challenges they have. As we equip people in these four areas we introduce other significant biblical truth like the designs of men and women, the judgments, the image of God, and how different men and women are. But the starting point is always equipping people with the knowledge and ability to apply the foundation and use the four tools in a way that supports them, their spouse, and the longevity of the relationship.

All our teaching employs the amazing grace, love, and freedom found through walking with our savior Jesus Christ, the ultimate example of pursuing the best for others.

Our hopes and prayers are with you, that you will take what you have learned from this book and small group discussions and employ them to build and sustain GR8 Relationships!

STUDY GUIDE

Scripture Meditation

Time: 30 minutes a day

Each day read and meditate on one of the scriptures listed below, or as directed by your session leader. Follow these steps.

1. Get in a quiet place without distraction.
2. Play a praise song and just listen to the words.
3. Ask God to reveal His heart and meaning to you as you read the scriptures.
4. Write your reflections below or in your journal.
5. Read the scriptures daily so you receive maximum revelation.

medical	spiritual
STEP ONE: Stop the bleeding	Face your humanity
STEP TWO: Clean the wound	Overlook revenge
STEP THREE: Apply antibiotic	Renew your mind
STEP FOUR: Cover the wound	Give it up, grasp it no more
STEP FIVE: Change the dressing regularly	Apply your decision
STEP SIX: Look for signs of infection	Validate and verify your decision
STEP SEVEN: Enjoy healing	Enjoy healing and freedom

Who's to Blame?

REFLECTIVE QUESTIONS

Think about how content in this book applies to your own life and answer the questions below.

- Describe some situations where you notice your *Flashing ME*. How did those times impact relationships?

FLASHING ME EPISODE	HOW IT IMPACTED RELATIONSHIPS

- What can you do to make sure you pursue the best for others patiently, kindly, sacrificially, and unconditionally?

_____

_____

_____

_____

_____

- How can you apply this scripture to your life right now?

   For where envy and self-seeking exist, confusion and every evil thing are there.

   James 3:16, NKJV

_____

_____

_____

_____

_____

What Breaks Down?

REFLECTIVE QUESTIONS

- Describe a situation where your feelings were untruthful to you. For example, a scary movie or a business situation, where you were unsure of your status.

_____

_____

_____

_____

_____

_____

- Think about a strong feeling you experienced recently. What were you reacting to?

_____

_____

_____

_____

_____

_____

- Describe a relationship where you do not experience freedom. Explain why.

_____

_____

_____

_____

_____

- Describe a current or past situation where you had difficulty forgiving someone one. Determine and describe what made it hard for you to forgive them.

_____

_____

_____

_____

_____

- What holds you back from confessing to others? How can you improve?

_____

_____

_____

_____

_____

What is the Best ME?

REFLECTIVE QUESTIONS

- Describe an attitude you need to change. For example, your attitude toward a friend. What do you need to do to begin to transform your feelings, emotions and ultimately attitude?

_____

_____

_____

_____

_____

- Over the next month, any time you feel like you did not have any options in a situation, record the situation in a journal. Then stop and think hard about a different choice you could have made. What difference would it have made in the situation?

_____

_____

_____

_____

_____

- Over the next month, think about any sin you need to confess. Take yourself through the Steps of Confession. Record your feelings of freedom after confessing.

_____

_____

_____

_____

_____

_____

Forgiveness Exercise

- Write down on a small card or piece of paper the name of the person you want to forgive, and what is being forgiven.
- Take the card and go to a quiet place.
- Kneel and place the card in your hands palms up. Hold the card up to heaven. Pray to the Lord in your own words what you have written on the card and tell Him you are forgiving them, and you want Him to take this event from you.
- Pray whatever else you desire about the event and when you finish write the date and time on the card.
- Put the card in a safe place to remind you that you have forgiven the person, or throw the card away if there is a chance the person might see it.
- But remember the date somehow. Now you have a date, a memorial to remind you that you forgave them.

TOOLS

The following tools will enable you to understand yourself and your spouse and how you can work together to handle conflict. The videos listed below are a part of the video course that corresponds to the information in this book. Completing all the courses will be instrumental for you to find FREEDOM!

You can find all these tools (and many more) on our website www.GR8relate.com at the TOOLS tab.

Kolbe Assessment https://gr8relate.com/kolbe

You can trust the validity and accuracy of the Kolbe instrument to show you your strengths and instincts. The Kolbe also helps you easily see and understand how the strengths and talents of one person may not be considered as strengths by another. This critical information will help you bridge the gap between reality and your expectations of them. Once you complete the assessment, you will receive detailed reports that will help you understand your strengths and talents and how to use your strengths in a complementary way with your spouse, family member, or friend's strengths. By understanding your instincts you can more easily discuss your differences, laugh about them, and develop ways to deal with them.

The *Thomas-Kilman Conflict Mode Instrument* (TKI) https://gr8relate.com/tki

The TKI is the world's best-selling instrument for understanding conflict. It helps you see that conflict can be beneficial and useful, instead of thinking conflict as bad. You will be provided detailed information on effectively using all five conflict modes: competing, collaborating, compromising, avoiding, and accommodating.

The *Fundamental Interpersonal Relations Orientation-Behavior*™ (FIRO-B®). https://gr8relate.com/firob

The FIRO-B helps you understand how you interact at work and personal life. This easy-to-complete-assessment will provide critical insights into how an individual interacts with others. This personality instrument measures how you typically behave with others and how you expect them to act toward you.

Individual Videos

Ten Second Summary of GR8 Relationships – https://vimeo.com/164152149
Am I Making This About Me? – https://vimeo.com/164736178
Two Circles – https://vimeo.com/164736180
What Is the Order? – https://vimeo.com/168487959
God the Model for Freedom – https://vimeo.com/168492029
Step 1 – Face Their Humanity – https://vimeo.com/169007008
Confession Insights – https://vimeo.com/169024281

Go Deeper

This book series is designed to help you start finding Freedom in all your relationships. If you want to dig deeper, we've got more! Go here: https://gr8relate.com/video-courses/ These are our FREE courses. You will learn more about your relationships. And if you like what you see, please help us Pay It Forward to help others gain Freedom in their Relationships.

Forms

The following forms will be useful tools as your work through your relationships. You can copy these as you need them. You can also find these and other useful tools at www.gr8relate.com. Click on the Tools tab.

Six Guidelines When Confessing

Right Attitude

- Always think of them as more important than you – (Philippians 2:3-4)
- Have NO expectations about changing them
- Go with a heart that knows you wronged them and will confess your wrong, no strings attached
- Be Humble & Defenseless
- Believe Resolution is Possible
- Slow Your Emotions Down!

> **Philippians 2:3-4**: Let nothing be done through selfish ambition or conceit, but in lowliness of mind let each esteem others better than himself. Let each of you look out not only for your own interests, but also for the interests of others.

Right Words

- When confessing be careful of the words you use
- If you have not confessed to God, you will not like using the words that must be used here
- A Pattern for Right Words.

> ### A Pattern for Right Words
> - AGREE: I was wrong when I (describe attitude and actions)
> - ACKNOWLEDGE: I realize that this has hurt you (and others)
> - ADMIT: I regret my actions and repent before God and you
> - ANNOUNCE: I plan to (state actions) to help me not do that again
> - Thank you for listening. If there are other items that need to be cleared up, I am willing to discuss those also, now or later.

Right Method

- A personal visit is probably the best overall
- A phone call can be very helpful for tough issues
- A letter is least preferred

Right Time

- Is the time convenient for the other person?
- Is it a time when you would not likely be interrupted?
- What is a danger when thinking of the right time?

Right Communication Style

- Deal gently even if they are not gentle with you
- Slow the emotions down!
- Prepare before and even role-play gentleness
- Use speech seasoned with grace
- Take 100% Responsibility to Communicate
  - Communication is cursed
  - Communication is delicate
  - Understand first, then disagree
  - Don't assume you will be understood
  - Look at them during conversation
  - Speak the "Truth in Love" (Eph. 4:15)

> **Galatians 6:1** Brethren, if a man is overtaken in any trespass, you who are spiritual restore such a one in a spirit of gentleness, considering yourself lest you also be tempted.
>
> **James 3:17** But the wisdom that is from above is first pure, then peaceable, gentle, willing to yield, full of mercy and good fruits, without partiality and without hypocrisy.
>
> **Colossians 4:6** Let your speech always be with grace, seasoned with salt, that you may know how you ought to answer each one.
>
> **Proverbs 15:1** A soft answer turns away wrath, But a harsh word stirs up anger.
>
> **Proverbs 6:16-19** These six things the Lord hates, Yes, seven are an abomination to Him: A proud look, a lying tongue, hands that shed innocent blood, a heart that devises wicked plans, feet that are swift in running to evil, a false witness who speaks lies, and one who sows discord among brethren.

Right Meeting Guidelines

- Create handout (see Meeting Guidelines) for the parties that will be participating
- Ask permission of the other party to send the guidelines to them
- In some situations, select a trusted, wise third party to facilitate
- Use the guidelines even if no third party present
- Look up all the verses in the Meeting Guidelines prior to meeting to refresh your mind to truth

51 Relationship Principles

1. Think of others as important, in fact, more important than you.

2. 3 Simple Guidelines; 3 Simple Questions
   a. Do what is right. Will I do what is right?
   b. Be trustworthy. Will I commit to doing my best?
   c. Do to others as you would have them do to you. Will I pursue the good of and serve others more than myself?

3. Freedom in relationships does not mean license; it primarily involves being a real person and letting others be themselves.

4. Freedom blossoms relationships: control and manipulation limit them.

5. Freedom in marriage allows each person to operate in their design.

6. If people are not free to be themselves around you, then, most likely, your relationships are all about YOU.

7. When freedom and choice are not in a relationship, someone is being controlled (dominated or manipulated).

8. When you cannot be yourself in a relationship, the relationship will become intolerable.

9. When freedom and choice are in a relationship, the whole person (good & bad) is accepted.

10. When you are tense, angry, frustrated, or irritated, it often means someone is not doing the job you assigned them.

11. Your happiness is a lousy job to assign to anyone or anything. Why let someone else control you that way?

12. When you take things personally, you are not operating in freedom.

13. Without freedom in a relationship, someone will be a fake, hypocrite, or liar.

14. If a relationship must satisfy you, you are walking down the manipulation trail (You are saying NO to the relationship and making the relationship about you; freedom is limited).

15. Relationships happen in reality, in real-time, with real people.

16. No one owes you anything in a relationship.

17. The closer you are to change, the greater will be the resistance.

18. To the degree we deny our issues, we will find a scapegoat on which to dump them.

19. Victims are focused on getting their circumstances and those around them to change, not on changing themselves.

20. Victims must be rescued; they are dependent on circumstances or others' changes to make them happy.

21. Draw a line in the sand and create a new past.

22. Give people more than they expect cheerfully.

242 Spring Park Drive, Ste A   Midland, Texas 79705   Phone: 432-682-6823   https://gr8relate.com   Email: info.gr8relate@gr8grp.com

Pursuing Their BEST
– in Work, in Life, in Love

Conflict RESOLVED BluePrint

Remember 4+3+2 Essentials

4 Critical Principles	3 Cardinal Rules	2 Skills	5 Styles
·**RELATIONSHIPS**: WE, not just ME ·**FUTURE**: The Past is OVER ·**FREEDOM**: Don't try to change them ·**KINDNESS**: Kindness instead of winning	·**SLOW** the emotions down ·**TALK** until a solution is found ·Seek **TWO**-sided solutions	·Listening ·Asking Questions	·Accommodating ·Avoiding ·Collaborating ·Competing ·Compromising

Evaluate the Conflict: Questions...

Conflict	You	Them	Meeting
·What is it about? ·What are the components? ·How will it impact the relationship? ·Will we 1) battle until the other changes? 2) disagree and end relationship, 3) disagree and keep relationship 4) resolve and keep relationship 5) resolve and end the relationship	·What was my role, contribution? ·What resolution do I want? ·What are my needs, goals? ·Do I need them? ·Are my expectations reasonable? ·What misperceptions might they have of me?	·Am I defining them by their negative behavior? ·What are their needs? ·Do I understand their side? ·What misperceptions might I have of them? ·What buttons do they have?	·What Method? ·What Time? ·What Location?

Set the Ground Rules

3 Cardinal Rules	General Rules		Good Values
·**SLOW** the emotions down ·**TALK** until solution is found ·Seek **TWO**-sided solutions	·Be Clear ·"Speak to the center of the room" ·No attacking or blaming ·One person speaks at a time	·Look at each other when speaking ·All ideas as valid when presented ·Build on each other's ideas ·Explore each idea	·Be Fair ·Be Honest ·Be Responsible ·Be Respectful ·Be Considerate

Open the Conversation

Open and honest about seeking a solution	Partner with them; create a WE atmosphere	Encourage options through shared effort	Narrow the scope – agreement on everything is not required

Listen and Clarify

Focus only on them	Observe what they say	Seek facts with good questions	Summarize; check what you heard	Summarize often	Seek Permission

Value and Seek Options

Criteria for Good Options	Meets one or more shared needs	Meets one or more needs not incompatible with other party	Potential to improve future relationship	Can be supported by all parties
Uncover Options	Seek their options first	Learn from the past	Keep your ears open!	

Establish A Solution

·WE (2-sided solutions) ·Thinking (Slow emotions down) ·Facts (talk)	·Focus on shared needs ·Increase the size of the pie	Behavior specific	Document it

Decide to Follow-up

242 Spring Park Drive, Ste A   Midland, Texas 79705   Phone: 432-682-6823   https://gr8relate.com   Email: support@gr8relate.com

Pursuing their BEST
~ in Work, in Life, in Love

Meeting Guidelines

Be Thankful in Prayer
- Thank God for the conflict – 1 Thessalonians 5:18
- Accept that God has been and is at work in the conflict – Genesis 50:20, Romans 8:28
- Praise God for allowing the sin. Sin is the root problem, not the other person and not God – James 4:1, Romans 6:12-13
- Accept confession and forgiveness are God's answer to conflict
- Ephesians 4:32, Colossians 3:13, 1 Peter 3:8-9

Be Humble
- James 4:6; 1 Peter 5:6-7
- Allow God's grace to permeate your lives – James 4:10
- Recognize both of you are depraved apart from Christ – Romans 3:10-12, Ephesians 2:1-6
- Each of you accepts personal responsibility in the conflict. (Offer no defense. Pride is defensive.)

Be Just & Merciful
- Micah 6:8

Be Gentle
- Deal gently with each other – Galatians 5:22, James 3:17
- Consider the other person as more important than yourself; Philippians 2:3-4
- Do not try to change the other person. (You are responsible for YOU. Pride causes us to focus on their faults.)

Be Gracious
- Use speech seasoned with grace
- Colossians 4:6, Proverbs 15:1, 6:16-19

Be Considerate
- Ephesians 4:15, Proverbs 21:10

Be Renewed
- Christ's life (your new life) and the Holy Spirit's energy are the keys to any resolution
- Galatians 2:20, 5:16, 24-25; 2 Corinthians 5:17

Be Clear
- Speak about the problem, not the person
- Use the "Speak to the Center of the Room" communication style. Pick an object to represent the problem and talk about it, even point at it

Be Honest About Facts & Feelings

Use "I + feel + when" technique

> ### "I + feeling word + when"
> 1. Begin conversation with a qualifier
>   - "I want to tell you how I feel"
>   - "I am not asking you to agree with me"
>   - Never use BUT after those statements (can be manipulative)
> 2. State your feelings ("I am really upset")
> 3. Always use observable behavior
>   - "I was hurt when you didn't speak to me last night."
>   - NOT, "You always are hurting me"
> 4. Reframe or "mirror" what is said
>   - "What I hear you saying..."
>   - "I am not sure that I understand, but let me tell you what I heard."

Love's Current Reality

Score yourself on how you relate to your SPOUSE or a SPECIAL relationship. Use a 1 to 10 scale, where 1 is worst, and 10 is best (10 = Never or Always in the statements below)		
1.	I suffer long; I am patient— I always endure evil, injury, and provocation, without being filled with resentment, bitterness, or grudges	
2.	I am kind—I always am gracious toward and do good for others	
3.	I do not envy, I am not jealous—I never compare myself to others, never suspect unfaithfulness, never feel inferior because of comparison	
4.	I do not brag or boast—I never have an "I" problem, never judge or act like I am better than others	
5.	I am not puffed up, proud—I never call attention to myself, never puffed up about myself or my possessions	
6.	I do not behave rudely—I am always courteous, respectful, considerate, chivalrous, gallant	
7.	I do not seek my own—I am never self-seeking or self-absorbed, never have to have it my way	
8.	I am not provoked—I am never easily angered or react to what others are doing to me, always operate on Godly values	
9.	I think no evil—I never keep a list or think of wrongs done to me	
10.	I do not rejoice in evil—I never condone or tolerate evil or wrongdoing and never rejoice when it happens	
11.	I rejoice in truth—I am always delighted to see truth win, delighted when truth is shared with me when I have been wrong, delighted to get constructive criticism	
12.	I bear all things—I always protect others, never share their faults when speaking to others	
13.	I believe all things—I always trust, never suspicious, assuming, or reluctant to believe the best about others	
14.	I hope all things—I always hope for the best without controlling or manipulating	
15.	I endure all things—I always persevere in good and tough times, and I never feel compelled to talk about my problems	

Using the above information, identify 1 or 2 items you would like to enhance. Write an action you could regularly take this month to help you score higher next time.

242 Spring Park Drive, Ste A   Midland, Texas 79705   Phone: 432-682-6823   https://gr8relate.com   Email: support@gr8grp.com

ENDNOTES

1   https://gr8relate.com/hermann-louie? content
    adapted from online video.

2   *The Art of Forgiving*, Louis B. Smedes, Ballentine
    Books, 1997.

3   *Changed into His Image*, Jim Berg, BJU Press, 2018.